GRAZING IN THE LIGHT: THE POWER OF THE MIND

Innocent Onyedikachi
Nnaoma Nwachukwu

authorHOUSE®

AuthorHouse™
1663 Liberty Drive
Bloomington, IN 47403
www.authorhouse.com
Phone: 833-262-8899

Published by AuthorHouse 12/01/2022

ISBN: 978-1-6655-7261-3 (sc)
ISBN: 978-1-6655-7260-6 (e)

Print information available on the last page.

This book is printed on acid-free paper.

CONTENTS

FOREWORD

The book, Grazing in the Light: the Power of the Mind, is a handbook written in a simple format. It is able to take one's thoughts afar field. It transports the reader across the threshold of stormy and windy waves of life. One soars in it without losing a breath. Once picked, it is up for being devoured with relish. The piece of pie will be best enjoyed in the act of eating since one bite will lead to a total consumption of the whole. The author has made it handy and precise for an easy intellectual banquet for the reader.

The work primarily makes evident that the journey towards success in this world and towards heaven is not an easy one. It is one that passes through tough, darkened and inadequately illumined tunnels. Inside these subways, there are obstacles, sufferings, discomforts, etc. It describes the tour as "the royal rumble battle between the darkness and the light."

However, it also insists that the tourist's steadfastness, renewed mindset and positive thinking assuredly see him or her through. Following the scriptures, the author asserts that the journey involves a battle which is not only against flesh and blood but against powers and principalities.

The work highlights that life's journey has never been an easy battle. This, accordingly, is because the prince of darkness and his agents are poised for rampage. They know that their time is almost up. They seek to throw in the deceit and malady of evil-living. This is in order to entangle their prey in the web of confusion, desperation, apathy, discouragement and the likes. But God's infinite grace and protection for the sons of light are unshakeable. His presence, as light, gives courage and joy every day. Therefore, in the midst of difficulties and untold dangers of life, traceable to the evil one and his agents, people can still graze in the light. By this they will debunk and dethrone the evil plans of the enemy and be making a living once they are walking in light or have faith that "nothing is impossible before God." Christ has made this abundantly clear.

In this delightful grazing in the light, the mind plays an important part. It is the center of human activities. Thinking positively and having a right mindset gets the winning ball rolling. It offers one the resistance and tenacity to overcome artificial challenges. However, the human mind itself, to be a winner must seek to be sacred. It has to imitate the sacred heart of Jesus. This implies that it has to be without impurity, without hatred, divested of envy, and devoid of other ill-manners. It should be a dwelling place of God, the tabernacle of the most High and a wonderful abode of spiritual and holy thoughts. It must strive to be free from prejudices and all devilish covens.

Finally, the book underlines that all persons are born with goals in life. Each human being is born to win and heaven should be his or her final bus stop. Thus, all human efforts should be channeled towards making heaven. Without it, one might suffer great losses and may throw in the trowel. Accepting that plight would plunge one into the domain of darkness. This is where the devil and his agents are found and will inhabit forever. This is the condition that the author wants his readers to be spared from, starting already in this life.

I recommend the book to anyone who loves to bask in the sunlight of a good intellectual, socio-religious read. Beyond every form of darkness in life, God loves and Cares for you. Enjoy the light from the reading.

Rev Fr DR Anthony C Dimkpa
Lecturer and Vice Rector Seat of Wisdom Seminary Owerri.

INTRODUCTION

Light is a strong element needed in everyday life. It is an anti -darkness, a "conditio sine qua non" for a good living. Medically speaking, light is needed for bodily nourishment. It fights depression and other bodily diseases and cannot cohabit with darkness not withstanding how strong darkness may seem or exert its power. One of the clear evidences of this, is what I may call the "Royal rumble" of the eclipse of the sun where darkness always puts a fight to light. It reacts negatively and tries to get hold of the sun and its brightness but never in the annals of history has it succeeded.

Light pierces every thick darkness and remains the king and source of natural photosynthesis for plants, colorful array of fruit and a symbolic catalyst for human survival. It is antithetical to the thesis of darkness. In fact, the sons of light radiate like the sun. They are highly spirited and abhor any filthy elements that can obscure the brightness of the light.

Grazing in the light amidst darkness buttresses this fact. This book exposes the fact that darkness is an ugly and inimical element that tends to create confusion and crisis not only on our way to heaven but also on our human relationship and exploits.

Darkness is an agent of deception especially metaphorical darkness, a mirage that destroys human progress and relationship and when it takes over human mind, the result is dramatic: depression, suicide, homicide, fratricides and the likes.

It is indeed an enemy of man though some people argue that it helps the body to relax during sleep (i.e., those who think or believe that one can only have a sound sleep when the artificial light is turned off). We shall come to this point later, that is why I called darkness a philosophical mirage, a phantasmagoria, the bane of human progress, because only the strong comprehend its capacity to make one gullible and generate illusion. We must vehemently defend the fact that the Sons of light showcase goodness, empathy, sympathy and so on while the Sons of darkness jubilate over human failures; they are part of the mayhem that bedevil society today.

Grazing in the light amidst darkness as book x-rays also the power of the mind to fight evil. The mind in fact is like a cup. It is what one puts into it that the person will drink. It can habour darkness if one fills it in with darkness and it can fight darkness if the person constructs and reconstructs it to function in that manner.

The mind is a voracious and unquenchable object of knowledge. It filters evil when managed well and dispels darkness that can becloud human knowledge. We will elaborate this factor later. Meanwhile, let us explicate the terms of our discussion.

CHAPTER ONE

EXPLICATION OF TERMS

1.1 The Term Light and its Etymology

Etymologically, the term "Light" traces its origin from the old English word "*lēoht*", "*liht*" (noun and adjective) "*līhtan*" (verb), of Germanic origin, related to Dutch *Licht* and German *Licht*, from an Indo - European root shared by Greek *leukos* "white" and Latin Lux "light."[1] In the Italian language it is

---

[1] Cf. Google Dictionary, definizioni de Oxford Languages. You will find this dictionary on internet via google. *Lux* is the Latin root also. It defines clearly what light is as that which radiates and dispels darkness. There is joy and dazzling of outfit in the presence of light. Even the Italian word "luce" clarifies this concept. That is why

called "*luce*." It is the dispenser of holiness, wholeness, healthiness and wellness.

Religiously speaking, it refers to God though it was created by Him. It is analogical to His nature. It is through His spoken word that light came to be. "And the earth was without form, and void, and darkness was upon the face of the deep. And the spirit of God moved upon the face of the waters. And God said, let there be light and the was light, and God saw the light, and it was good and God divided the light from darkness" (Genesis 1:3 KJV). Therefore, light is a pure and undiluted element created by God to dispel darkness. He even did the separation Himself knowing fully well the antagonistic nature of darkness because He is "omniscient" (all knowing). He knows that light bequeaths goodness and it is in ever-green harmony with His Nature. It is good to know that the second Person of the Most Holy Trinity is holistically classified as light, the "Logos" (the Word). We will delve in detail into it when we will be talking about

---

St Lucy is seen as the protectress of eyes because her name depicts light and we see light through the eye.

the subheading "the Light shines in the dark..." in the gospel of John chapter 1.

Light is necessary in the activities of man. In ancient times, the primitive man *homo sapiens* used to gather stones to create light. He would scratch the surface of the two stones together. It was a means of survival. Man in state of nature was not only brutish and wolf to man as the philosopher, Thomas Hobbes would say. He was also creative and agile. He was able to discover light as the source of energy in cooking and a vital means of shriveling and crisping of human wears and bodily energy. Scientifically, the meeting of two hot air masses creates light. This is what today we call lightening. Whenever, it strikes, it not only creates light but also dispels darkness and unravels the devilish amulets of the enemy. Thus, it is antithetical and inimical to the thesis of evil. Light as an element has a myriad of sources. A navigation on them, will enrich our knowledge and meaning of light.

1.1.1 Various Sources of Light

There are various sources of light – natural and artificial. A few examples of natural light sources include God, the sun, the stars and the likes while a few examples of artificial light sources include light bulbs, lamp posts and televisions. Without light sources, we could not see the world around us. We will be taping and gallivanting in darkness. Lets us now peruse through the aforementioned sources starting with the creator Himself – God.

1.1.1.1 God the Almighty

We know biblically that there are 3 persons in one God – three persons sharing one substance. The nature of the Holy Trinity, God the father, God the son and God the Holy spirit is enigmatic. God the father is the creator. He created all things from nothing. God the son is the "*logos*" (the word, the *verbum* through whom all things were created while God the Spirit sanctifies. Every one of their actions is the action of God. However, they work together in love and light as it is in the book Genesis: "Then

God said, "Let us make man in our image, after our likeness.. (Gen 1: 26 RSV)." The phrase "let us" shows that they work hand in glove and they are the primary source of light. In fact, they are light themselves because "nemo dat quod non habet" (No one gives what he does not have). If they were not source of light or if there was no light in them, they wouldn't have created light. Thus, they are the originator of light and the Son "Dei verbum" (the word of God) would say, Again Jesus spoke to them, saying, "I am the light of the world; he who follows me will not walk in darkness, but will have the light of life (Jn 8:12 RSV)." "I am in the father and the father is in me." He is in harmony with the father, and in God there is no iota of darkness. We can buttress this point further with the scene of the transfiguration in the Bible where the cloak of God the Son became so dazzling that nothing on earth could be used to compare with its brightness. He was totally enrolled in light (cf. Mathew 17:1-8, mark 9: 2-8, Luke 9: 28-36).

we must all struggle to embrace light and it is rooted and founded on the teaching of God in His creation: "Let there be light and there was light." One cannot talk about the "Theophany" (from Greek "*theophaneia*" appearance of God) without mentioning light. Even day light has its significance. This brings us to the second point, the sun as the source of light.

1.1.1.2 The Sun

Astronomically, the sun is a star round which the earth orbits. It shines from beyond a cloudless sky. The Earth draws its light from the sun while revolving around it. It is a heart line source of natural light. History has it that no human being has ever approached the sun because of the excruciating nature of its heat. Man in his exploits as recorded has visited many planets but has never ventured the going to the sun due to its temperature and the impending danger of losing his life. It is a danger zone. Some have likened it to be the creator himself due the fierce and enigmatic stories told about sun.

Biologically both living things and non – living things enjoy the effects of the sun. It is a mother that showers the earth the vital energy that is needed for its survival. Its energy is natural and not artificial. It does not have easily identifiable boundaries like rocky planets as our mother earth does. Rather it is composed of layers made up almost entirely of hydrogen and helium.

Let us not drift from our argument by talking about the composition of the sun. We are only interested in the fact that it is a natural source of light for human beings, animals and plants. We are all beneficiaries of its light. This will bring us to the third natural source light – the stars.

1.1.1.3 The Stars

The stars irradiate light and energy that are natural and bring man fulfilment. I could remember my childhood experience here, when we would look forward every night to folk tales from Mama and Papa. We would not only listen with keen interest to their lovely stories but also look forward to communal dialectical choruses and plays. Of course, the meeting point was always under the tree while we enjoyed the full moon and the light of the twinkling stars. We would make sure that we hurried over our domestic chores and waited for the brittle and frangible stars Cruise This appointment was never missed. It was fixed, eccentric and picturesque.

In other words, the light of the stars was and is still a clamoring and glamouring opportunity for reunions and meetings for families and age grades. Without the stars our homes at night constitute our graves, hide – outs and dungeons for the wicked. This is because the sons of darkness prefer to showcase their *modus operandi* and *modus vivendi* when there is no light, normally in the night where there is absence of light of the stars and the sun.

On the other hand, let us talk about the artificial sources of light though not in detail as done about the natural source of light. They include: Electricity and fire. They are not natural, they are man-made. Little wonder, a Philosopher like Battista Mondin holds that man is "a bundle of possibilities," because through his ingenuity he has been able to invent many things keeping strictly to the injunction of God, "Be fruitful and multiply, and fill the earth and subdue it;

and have dominion over the fish of the sea and over the birds of the air and over every living thing that moves upon the earth." (Gen 1: 28 RSV).

Man is capable of many things but many a times the small man in man – the ego seems to take upper hand. That is why man is sycophantic, hypothetical and manipulative. These egoistic tendencies lead man to prefer darkness to light. This is one of the reasons the ancient Greek philosopher Socrates states: "man know thyself." This is because a total submissiveness to the ego or human id can lead to human weakness and many emotional break downs. Darkness is one of the byproducts of the ego. The question now is what is "darkness"? Is it preferable to light?

1.2 What Darkness Is

The simplest definition of darkness is a total absence of light, a state of being dark. Some argue as I mentioned above that darkness begets a sound sleep. According to the proponents of this tenet, some people cannot sleep well except where there is darkness. This raises a tough eye brow: does it mean that those people are sick or children of darkness? Does it mean that darkness is preferred to light?

This is absolutely not correct. It is only a psychological state just like some people would panic and would not like to sleep in dark rooms. It is only a state of the mind. Therefore, this position remains porous as an argument. Moreover, darkness is an element of God's creation which gradually made a quantum leap or shift from good to bad due the activities of evil men. Many bad people glory in darkness since it helps them to cover their evil deeds. In this regard, Mehmet Murat Idan asserts" when you find light, enjoy it, because there is more darkness than light in the universe[2]. We need to be aware of darkness and its principalities, light is much desirable, and in the words of Martin Luther king Jr "Darkness cannot drive out darkness: only light can do that. Hate cannot drive out hate, only love can do that"[3].

---

[2] Cf https://www.goodreads.com .Martin Luther King Jr's postulation shows also the relevance of light and its forceful effect on the hate, greed and other vices, it drives them away and establishes love and peace.

[3] Cf https://www.goodreads.com

Therefore, love and light go hand in glove while darkness runs contrary to their positive postulations.

Darkness invariably connotes desperation, marginalization, depression, evil, sin and all ugly verbal denotations which tantamount to human degradation and relegate human dignity to the background. It belongs to the people of the underworld and their agents.

2.1 Agents of Darkness

An outstanding agent of darkness is the devil or Lucifer from Italian word "Lucifero" which is coined from the Latin "lux" which means light bearer. He was once a light bearer before his egoistic tendencies misled him and threw him into panic. He was thrown down and in his despair and trauma, he started traumatizing the world. When the scripture talks about darkness it refers to a sinful path. Jesus is the light while Lucifer is the father of all liars and darkness.

Another name for Lucifer is Satan which is the English transliteration of a Hebrew word for adversary, the ancient human adversary, the tempter. In the bible Satan is cynical about disinterested human goodness. Throughout the New Testament Satan is referred to as the tempter (cf. Matthew 4:3), the ruler of the demons (cf. Matthew 12: 24), the god of this era (cf. 2 Corinthians 4:4), the evil one (cf. 1 John 5: 18) and a roaring lion (cf. 1 Peter 5:8). He is afraid of suffering alone in hell. So, in his cynical nature, he decided to build himself a kingdom, a web in which many souls have been entangled waiting for the final judgment.

Unfortunately, many keep on falling prey to him even till date. This is probably because of the euphoric and glaring taste of the world. Many have lost it and have followed the German philosopher, Friedrich Nietzsche who after seeing how people were suffering in the world without help proclaims the famous atheistic axiom "*Deus mortuus est*" (God is dead). Such people become the secondary agents of darkness: the unbelievers, those who live by the adage, "let us eat today for tomorrow we may die." They believe in absolute pragmatism, agnosticism and the negation of goodness. But time shall reveal the truth which is God, already revealed but neglected by unbelievers. The truth is that darkness cannot hold the light under siege. Light is un-coverable and unconquerable.

CHAPTER TWO

APHORISM OF LIGHT IN THE SACRED SCRIPTURE

2.1 Living in Light

Navigating and perusing through our explication of terms in chapter one, we have been able to understand and throw to limelight what light is and its sources. This little but substantial exposé will be our pathfinder as we delve into the glorious and heroic nature of man in the heavenly light. The sons of light are the sons of harvest. They will dazzle and glare like the stars in the sky, the bible says. They will renew their strength. They will spread their wings and soar like Eagles. They will run and will not get tired. They will walk and not lag behind (Isaiah 40: 31). Their footprints are golden. Their strength remains unwavered, green-grassy, leafy and pastoral. They will pasture in the midst of lions and other dreaded animals without panic. God Himself will be their light.

I remember encountering a young man and his family in one of my trips to Switzerland. He was so pious and God-fearing. He had pretty children all looking chubby and buxom. I was deeply moved to ask him about his journey to Switzerland because Switzerland is one of the toughest countries to penetrate in Europe. If you have no documents, even when you think that you have double-crossed the frontier warders, if you have not finally settled, you are still a clandestine. He narrated to me how God's grace saw him through. Even the immigration officers did not ask him any questions. It was a smooth ride. He was grazing in light amidst turbulences, pasturing and soaring in a willowy and sylph-like slop without trepidation because God has already lightened up the way. The child of God in this regard, becomes only a consumer of God's work but it does not mean that no hard work is required for this stride. It is the combination of faith and hard work because faith without good works is dead (cf. James 2: 26).

To be living in light means placing God in the first place. It means dislodging the human ego and allowing faith to penetrate the thickened darkness of hopelessness, desperation and the entanglement of the mind with unwanted infatuations of greedy, arrogant and malicious traits. It means moving in the spirit ("*Ruach*" in Hebrew while *pneuma* in Greek) because "*Ruach*" (the Spirit) penetrates the wall of heaven. It is that power that animates the body and encourages man to undertake unimaginable and ineffable adventures of life. Thus, moving in the spirit means moving in light.

Do we still remember the scenario of the Pentecost where the strong wind blew and the upper room where the apostles were, covered with light, the tongues of fire? The account reads thus: "When the day of Pentecost had come, they were all together in one place. And suddenly a sound came from heaven like the rush of a mighty wind, and it filled all the house where they were sitting. And there appeared to them tongues as of fire, distributed and resting on each one of them (Acts 2 RSV)." It is in similitude to theophany of the burning bush in the book of Exodus. I shall come to it later. To call the spirit, fire or light is not out of question. It is *ad rem* to our discussion. Little wonder the Catechism of the Catholic Church asserts: "It is true that beyond its proper name Spirit, which can also mean breath, air or wind, various symbols, including "fire" are used in the Bible to designate the Holy Spirit. These include: water of life, anointing, cloud and light, seal, hand, finger, dove, etc.[4]

God is light and living in the light means rejection of darkness, turning our backs against evil and its traumatic but glaring attractions. It is good to bear in mind that the devil does not go on pension. He does not rest. He is the father of wicked grin. His target is to destroy, exterminate and lead many souls to hell fire.

---

[4] Cf. Catechism of the Catholic Church, 694-700. This is a book that contains some doctrines of the catholic faith or teaching. Non Catholics may not be familiar with it. It has a lot to say on the event of the Pentecost and the word "Holy Spirit."

We cannot talk about living in the light without talking about "Metanoia," the Greek word for a transformative change of heart, especially a spiritual conversion. Thus, walking with God demands change of mindset, a total transformative attitude towards the sacred because darkness and light have no convergence. It is either that one is living in the light or the person is living in darkness. There is no room for mediocrity because in discipleship, a middle state is obtainable. The bible says that it is either you are hot or cold otherwise you will be thrown out (cf. Revelation 3:15). Change of heart means a total rejection of the devil and his modus operandi, and setting the mind where there is fullness of joy – the heavenly throne of the Lord Almighty.

Meanwhile, sons of light are light bearers. Living in the light means bearing the light – light of salvation; bringing joy where there is agony; bringing hope where is desperation; bringing peace where there is crisis and confusion; finally bringing light where there is darkness and depression. It is a clarion call for total self-giving, knowing full well that He who called us is faithful and in him there is no darkness. He is a covenant keeping God.

2.2 God as Dispenser of Light

We draw our reflection here from the book of Exodus. This is one of the five books of Moses called in Hebrew the "Torah." Here we are going to reflect on theophany – the appearance of God in form light vis a vis, the mystery of the burning Bush and God revealing himself as Jahveh, the "I am who I am." But before we delve into this explanation, let us know a brief the history of our protagonist here- Moses.

He is certainly the most outstanding human figure of the Hebrew Bible- the Christian Old testament. His childhood presented in Exodus2, is marked by the lot of his people, the Israelites, who were then under slavery in Egypt. With the rest of the male-children of his generation, he is condemned to death even before his birth. Pharaoh had in fact decreed "Every son that is born to the Hebrews you shall cast into the Nile, but you shall let every daughter live"(Ex 1,22). In this regard, Moses becomes a "Patron saint" of all those who are condemned for a crime they never committed, or in any case, without a chance to give their own version of the cause brought up against them[5]. Helpless before the cruel condemnation, Moses's mother first tries to hide the child, but later after three months she is no longer able to do so, but has to submit to the decree of Pharaoh. In her submission to this decree, she hands Moses over, not to the Egyptians but directly to the river. It is as

---

[5] Nwachukwu F.A., The courage to Change. Nairobi: Paulines Pub. 2003 p. 40 ff. He is also the patron of the victims of ingratitude. His early life confronts us with a number of questions and observations. How often do we find ourselves in fortunate situations in spite of ourselves, that is, without earning them through our own efforts? Do we, in such circumstances, forget our origins and former colleagues, or do we have the courage and humility to still remain in solidarity with them? Further, there may be occasions when we too find ourselves victims of ingratitude, betrayed by the same persons we have sought to help. Or still, sometimes we may even have been made to lose almost everything in very sincere efforts to help others. Such was the story of Moses, the young (cf Nwachukwu, F.A., The Courage to Change, Nairobi: Paulines Pub., 2003, p.40 ff

though she trusts more "in the kindness of the natural forces than in the human executioners of Pharaoh's orders". In other words, Moses' mother takes a basket and places the child therein, a final resting place for him- his casket and tomb. The mother must be heart-broken. Yet one notices a strong ray of hope in her mind. She believes in God as the true light which drives away darkness and its agents. Though her child may suffer a lot at the heart of darkened water, if God does not say, it is over, it is not yet over. Every life belongs to God. Leaving him beside the water, may be a symbol of his "second birth- baptism" since it is a necessary factor to be a Christian and make heaven too.

The mother left the scene, while the sister stood at a distance to watch the imminent "end" of her brother, since her mother has left in silenc to contemplate and ruminate over the whole scenario. Some biblical scholars like Fortunatus Nwachukwu, is of the opinion that " the identity of the sister is not given. If she is Miriam (Num 26,59), then that name links her in some way to another Miriam(Mary) who, centuries later, would wait patiently while the new

Moses slept in his tomb"[6]. It must be stated that God never allowed her mother to be put to shame, He drove away all the darkness surrounded his birth and led him successfully to his destiny in light.

Thus, for many years, after the Israelites had sojourned in Egypt through the family of Jacob under the leadership of Joseph, darkness descended on them in Egypt. They suffered not only famine but also the tyrannic and cynical leadership of Pharaoh who would never listen to God and who led a pervasive and persuasive kingship. He could be recorded as an agent of darkness. He was everywhere with a cohesive, despotic and fascistic ruling spirit; he alone mattered.

The Israelites suffered humiliation, depression, anguish and desperation. They needed a light that can pierce the thick darkness of hatred, manipulation, child labour and abuse. God the father, the dispenser of light looked at their plight and decided to send

---

[6] Nwachukwu, F.A., The Courage to Change, Nairobi: Paulines, Pub., 2003, p.40 ff

The narrative makes sudden changes from sad to joy. The basket, the would have been casket and tomb of the child becomes womb from which the baby is born to a new life.

them a light bearer in the person of Moses. His appearance to Moses was theophanic. Moses saw the burning bush, the unquenchable light (*Das ewige LICHT* in German, the everlasting light cf. Ex 3-16). The abnormal spectacle of the "burning bush" catches Moses' curiosity. He wishes to get closer to examine better the riddle. "I will turn aside and see this great sight, why the bush is not burnt(Ex3,3)". Some biblical scholars are of the opinion that "the burning bush represents God's intention to destroy sin (darkness) and dispense grace (light). According to Chrysostom (347-407 CE) the bush represents the resurrection of the Jews and as the bush burned without being consumed, so also Jesus died but death did not overcome Him."[7] Fortunatus Nwachukwu holds that " the appearance of God by the means of natural forces, particularly: the wind, the fire or flame or light, the cloud, or weather, thunder and lightning are elements which reveal the mystery and strength of God. According to their nature, they can be quite destructive. It belongs to the nature of fire,

---

[7] Cf. http//www.scielo.org.za

for example to consume the thing which it burns".[8] However, Moses saw the contrary: the burning bush was not consumed by the flame of the fire. Therefore, something has broken the natural order; something mysterious and higher than nature. Buttressing this fact, Fortunatus Nwachukwu continues:

"When God is present, forces which are ordinarily destructive could lose their power to cause damage! That is true even with the "fire and flames", "the dark clouds" and the "thunders and lightening" of our daily life. If we bring God into them, they generally lose their power to wreak harvoc" [9].

Thus, as the bush was burning without being consumed, Moses was terrified. God called him and told him to put off his scandals, because he was on a holy ground.

"Moses, Moses!" And he said "Here am I." Then he said, Do not come near, put off your shoes from your

---

[8] Nwachukwu, F.A., The Courage to Change, Nairobi: Paulines, Pub., 2003, p.41 ff.

[9] Nwachukwu, F.A., The Courage to Change, Nairobi: Paulines, Pub., 2003, p.41 ff.

feet, for the place on which you are standing is holy ground" (Ex 3, 4-5).

"Light" here represents God, the holy God. It indirectly depicts light as a symbol of holiness. Little wonder that among Catholics, during baptism, burning candles are given to the baptized as a symbol of holiness and new creatures in God. In many Churches, candles are lit, or artificial lights are switched on to relay the fact that the "locus standi," the place of worship is a holy place. God dwells where there is "holy light" because not every light is holy. Some are used to invoke the devil by his agents. Christians must be well informed of this fact. There is deceit now in the world. The evil one is out on rampage. He has broken his chain and seriously looking for whom to devour. Let us have our holy light lit and get ready for fight. As the bible says "though the light shineth in the darkness, darkness cannot quench it" (John 1: 3ff). Even after God brought the Israelites out from bondage through Moses, the light bearer, He (God) did not abandon them. He accompanied them with His light. As the scripture says "on the morning of the third day there were thunder and lightning…on the mountain and a very trumpet blast, so that all the people in the camp trembled" (cf. Ex. 19: 16-20). Even in the desert toward the Promised Land, He led them with a pillar of cloud and fire. He never quenches the light of goodness on those He loves and trusts. Whosoever is led by the spirit is a son of light, as I said earlier. Though the light shines in the dark yet darkness has no power over it. We will throw more light on this now.

2.3 "The Light Shineth in Darkness…."

One of the biblical introductions that thrill me so much is the prologue of St John's gospel. It is a long but very enriching and encouraging introduction. It is neither sardonic nor satirical. I see it as a pure theology of the "*Verbum*" – the "*Logos*" and the revelation of divine mysteries. Let's have a full glance of it and thereafter we shall comment on it. It is the climax of our discussion here:

> In the beginning was the Word, and the Word was with God, and the Word was God. He was in the

beginning with God; all things were made through him, and without him was not anything made that was made. In him was life, [a] and the life was the light of men. The light shines in the darkness, and the darkness has not overcome it.

There was a man sent from God, whose name was John. He came for testimony, to bear witness to the light, that all might believe through him. He was not the light, but came to bear witness to the light.

The true light that enlightens every man was coming into the world. He was in the world, and the world was made through him, yet the world knew him not. He came to his own home, and his own people received him not. But to all who received him, who believed in his name, he gave power to become children of God; who were born, not of blood nor of the will of

> the flesh nor of the will of man, but of
> God. (John 1: 1-6 RSV).

This passage is really interesting. It discusses divine revelation – Christology, the enigma of hypostatic union, God the father revealing His Son to the world out of His love for mankind. An Italian cardinal and writer, late Mario cardinal Martini used two important words to describe this epochal theological movement of the "*Verbo*" (God the son). The two words are "*Essere*" (Being) e "*Tempo*" (time). This reminds me of the German Philosopher's – Martin Heideggerian – Being and Time in metaphysics. I see a similitude in the duo though this one is Theology while the latter is Philosophy. The "Essere" in question is God the Father, He is the "*Essere Perfettissimo*" (the Perfect Being) who could have remained hidden forever if He had wished but due to His being a loving father – THE LIGHT PER EXCELLENCE. His love for us made him to reveal Himself in the Person of His son Jesus Christ in "*Tempo*" (Time). This is the mystery of the incarnation. It is *the* manifestation or appearance of God the son. I may here borrow the Greek word "*Epifania*." In this case, it is no longer talking about the manifestation of Christ to the Magi; or His manifestation during his Baptism; or sometime in Cana in Galilee during His attendance to a wedding ceremony with His disciples and His Mother Mary. But I borrowed the word to talk about His manifestation to the entire world during His birth. The theology of incarnation of the Word of God (Verbum Domini) or Christology remains the heart of Christian theology. It is very vital to note this because the world was in absolute darkness; it was in sin; darkness beclouded human thinking and doing till the savior came. Thanks to God for His coming. If not, our fate would have remained the same. Darkness would have enveloped the whole universe. Man would have remained brutish – a wolf to his fellow man and the other negativities.

However, the coming of the "*Logos*" (the Word- the Light). The Love of God or the Beloved of God (*Agapetos* in Greek) was to bring joy and hope into the world because the aim was to liberate man from the den of darkness. But the irony was that the people for whom he came rejected Him. This is the essence of the brawny and sarcastic fight between the light and darkness. The Light shines in the darkness but the darkness fought the Light. The people fought the Savior. They wanted to extinguish the Light forever by killing Him. In fact, hanging Him on the cross was a means to mock Him, insult and humiliate Him without knowing that they were indirectly elevating Him. Thus, His people rejected Him as mentioned above. They preferred a thief to live during His prosecution but one good thing is that not all rejected him. The sons of light were on His part. As many as accepted Him, he gave the power to be called the sons of light. Put simply: "He was in the beginning with God; all things were made through him, and without him was not anything made that was made." (Jn 1: 2 RSV).

The question we need to ask ourselves now is this: where do I belong? Am I among those who accepted him or Am I among those who rejected Him? Some biblical scholars call those who rejected Him the black sheep and they are listed among the fallen angels.

2.3 The Fallen Angels

Satan, known as the devil, is an entity that seduces humans into sin or falsehood. Among the Jews, he is an agent subservient to God, typically regarded as a metaphor for the "*yetzer hara*" (evil inclination). Among Christians and Islam, he is seen as a fallen angel or "jinn" who rebelled against God. He was a light bearer before his rebellion. Nevertheless, God did not remove every power from him. He allows him temporary power over the fallen world. Thus, he has his cohorts – other deceiving agents. All those who intend to or who glory in sin are his agents: the men of underworld, the doers of evil and the sons of darkness.

The Bible was clear about the fall of Lucifer as a beautiful angel. The book of Ezekiel has this to say about him, though it would seem from the context of Ezekiel 28 that the first ten verses of this chapter are dealing with a human leader or hero but verse 11 through verse 19 refers to Lucifer. He is at the center of discussion. We shall support our argument with the book of revelation where exactly he was thrown down. Meanwhile, let us see what prophet Ezekiel has to say about this fallen hero of darkness:

> Moreover the word of the Lord came unto me, saying,
>
> Son of man, take up a lamentation upon the king of Tyrus, and say unto him, thus saith the Lord God; Thou sealest up the sum, full of wisdom, and perfect in beauty. Thou hast been in Eden, the garden of God; every precious stone was thy covering, the sardius, topaz, and the diamond, the beryl, the onyx, and the jasper, the sapphire, the emerald, the carbuncle and gold: the workmanship of thy tabrets and of thy pipes was prepared in thee in the day that thou wast created. Thou art the anointed cherub that covereth; and I have set thee so: thou wast upon the holy mountain of God; thou hast walked up and down in the midst of the stones of fire. Thou wast perfect in thy ways from the day

that thou wast created, till iniquity was found in thee.

By the multitude of thy merchandise they have filled the midst of thee with violence, and thou hast sinned: therefore I will cast thee as profane out of the mountain of God: and I will destroy thee, O covering cherub, from the midst of the stones of fire. Thine heart was lifted up because of thy beauty, thou hast corrupted thy wisdom by reason of thy brightness: I will cast thee to the ground, I will lay thee before kings, that they may behold thee.

Thou hast defiled thy sanctuaries by the multitude of thine iniquities, by the iniquity of thy traffick; therefore will I bring forth a fire from the midst of thee, it shall devour thee, and I will bring thee to ashes upon the earth in the sight of all them that behold thee. All they that know thee among the people shall be astonished at thee: thou shalt be a terror, and never shalt thou be any more. (Ezekiel 28 : 11- 19 KJV)

This point was further buttressed by the book of the prophet Isaiah thus:

"How art thou fallen from heaven, O Lucifer, son of the morning! How art thou cut down to the ground, which didst weaken the nations! For thou hast said in thine heart, I will ascend into heaven. I will exalt my throne above the stars of God. I will sit also upon the mount of the congregation, in the sides of the north. I will ascend above the heights of the clouds; I will be like the most High. Yet thou shalt be brought down to hell, to the sides of the pit. They that see thee shall narrowly look upon thee, and consider thee, saying: is this the man that made the earth to tremble, that did shake kingdoms; that made the world as a wilderness, and destroyed the cities

thereof; that opened not the house of
his prisoners?" (Isaiah 14: 12-17 KJV).

We cannot conclude our discussion here without mentioning the book of revelation 12-16 where the real war was waged by Lucifer against God and His faithful saints. It took off in the pre-mortal world, that is, in heaven and continues till date in this our mortal world. In spite of the fearful scenario described in these chapters, there are great reasons to be optimistic and joyful because he was vanquished and thrown into the den of torment and torture.

Moreover, our Lord Jesus assures us not to be afraid because He (i.e., Jesus) has conquered the world. In other words, He has won the ancient dragon. We are winners in the Lord if we choose to walk in the light. Meanwhile to be able to walk in the light, we need good mindsets. If the mind is clear and at rest, one sees clear and the nervous systems are relaxed.

CHAPTER THREE

DISCOVERING THE MIND AND ESTABLISHING A MINDSET

3.1 The Power of the Mind

The mind as an entity is likened to the brain. It is at the center of nervous system, the programmer of human activities. Without the mind, man is redundant and human daily coordination and activities are in jeopardy. Wikipedia calls it the "set of faculties responsible for mental phenomena". It is a center for human thought, imagination, memory, will and sensation. It is also responsible for various mental phenomena like perception, pain experience, belief, desire, intention and emotion.[10] In other words, the mind is the man and the man is the mind. They are inseparable. As a catalyst that sends information to other parts of the body, it needs accuracy, understanding and specification.

Thus, grazing in light amidst darkness as a book is regulated by the power of the mind. One cannot graze in light if the mind is feeble, dim and pale or if the mind is contaminated with evil thoughts. In fact, a turbulent mind, that is, a mind full of emotional storms and worries ends up reproducing anxieties, consternation, ill yearning desires and the likes. Such a mind is psychologically down. This can lead to depression because it is beclouded by darkness and emotional torments. In this regard, one is no longer himself or herself. One becomes the agent of the devil. The person would need psychological attention or spiritual healing. A darkened mind is a devil's workshop. The devil jubilates in our weaknesses. He rejoices when we are emotionally down. He makes merry when the mind is locked up or bedeviled by

[10] Cf. en.m.wikipedia.org. This dictionary is found on the internet. It partially defines the mind in non-holistic way.

hatred, selfishness, arrogance, envy, gluttony, greed, lust, sloth and other human vices. It is a state that calls for the Socratic axiom "man know thyself," as I mentioned before. This is because the outcome of this state is always dramatic if not followed conscientiously or perspicuously.

It must be stated clearly that God allows Satan some temporary powers. Thus, most of these human crises are his hand work. He hates seeing the sons of light in a happy mood. Some scholars like the atheists may argue that Satan does not exist and that what man suffers is traceable to the power of the mind or human thinking. This is feeble because not only adults fall sick but children are often diagnosed with strange sicknesses which in some cases, strong prayers and medical expertise resolve. Satan exists and he is behind human suffering. We will elaborate on this aspect in our further discussions.

Meanwhile, when we have a good mindset, when the mind is brightened up by good will, good intentions, marvelous and stupendous thoughts, the devil is set on the run. He goes into hiding. A happy heart is God's workshop. God dwells where there is serenity, tranquility and peace. If you are not happy, there is no way you can transmit happiness to other people. You can only fall back to devilish Coven, that is devil's cage.

Happiness comes from light, from reading the word of God, listening to music, having discussions and dialogues with people who love and welcome you and so on. A prayerful heart is a contented mind. It does not seek any vain glories but God's loving kindness. Such heart is meek. It is cheerful even when others are moody because the person with such heart believes strongly in the fact that our stay here is transitory. He knows that we are like people who live in the cave of the platonic allegory.

The Earth can be seen as a cave. Some believe that it is the real world. In this regard, they live and believe in the survival of the fittest. Man becomes wolf to man in their eyes just like in the state of nature by Thomas Hobbes. The Sons of light behave differently. They know that our lives here are short-lived. They are conscious of the heavenly race, knowing that someday they will leave this exilic cave and be in the real world. The best way to be a conqueror is to remain positive and focused.

3.2 Overcoming Failure: The Power of Positive Thinking

Man is born to win. He likes struggle even in the womb. Man struggles to come out. No human being likes failures or even being classified as a failure. Our natural inclination is to live lives worthy of emulation, lives of progress and to die leaving good legacies or with admirable footprints on the sand of time. Therefore, man is a resourceful being. He is a being endowed with rationality. He has been able to make gigantic strides and hyper-technological exploits, from the primitive stage to that of a global village and now to that of a global sitting room.

Man has been able to invent flying rockets, plying vehicles and so on. In his nature man is energetic, dynamic and zestful. Thanks to our Creator who loves and cherishes man. Little wonder, the Psalmist exclaims: what is man that you are mindful of him, the son of man that you care for him? You have made him little lower than the heavenly beings and crowned him with glory and honor… (cf. Psalm 8). Also, St Augustine knows that human achievements come from God. That is why he asserts:

> Great are you o Lord and exceedingly worthy of praise; your power is immense, and your wisdom beyond reckoning. And so we men, who are a due part of your creation, long to praise you – we also carry our mortality about with us, carry the evidence of our sin and with it the proof that you thwart the proud. You arouse us so that praising you may bring us joy, because you have made us and drawn us to yourself, and our heart is restless until it rests in you.[11]

In other words, no human analogy attributes failures to God. During my sojourn in Italy, I made many visits to ancient Rome precisely to the Vatican Museum.

---

[11] Augustine of Hippo, Confessions, in Crossroads initiative.com

One could see a lot of sculptures and paints which are byproducts of human ingenuities. Thus, failure is manmade, it can be termed also devilish. It is one of the instruments used by the devil to entangle man on the web of confusion, crisis and unfathomable bondage.

One of the best ways to conquer failure is to keep on trying and entrusting oneself to divine providence and intervention. He who falls and rises ten times has won a devilish battle ten times. At times, it may be a question of mindset. It, therefore, calls for a psychological alteration of the mind. It means that one makes a mental and psychological retrospect, go back to the root of the problem, challenge the background, face squarely the societal stigma and pressure, make amendments where necessary and above all, ask God for mental illumination and strength. This of course comes after one might have tried patiently for many years because patience is important and asking for divine illumination is also vital because our stormy and temperate trials at times may have divine undertone. A good example is the trial of Job in the Bible, though didactic. I would like to quote the first chapter of that book here because it is really interesting and it can open up our minds to know that at times our sufferings and trials are from God and could be short-lived, it goes thus:

> There was a man in the land of Uz, whose name was Job; and that man was perfect and upright, and one that feared God, and eschewed evil. And there were born unto him seven sons and three daughters. His substance also was seven thousand sheep, and three thousand camels, and five hundred yoke of oxen, and five hundred she asses, and a very great household; so that this man was the greatest of all the men of the east… Now there was a day when the sons of God came to present themselves before the Lord, and Satan came also among them.
>
> And the Lord said unto Satan, whence comest thou? Then Satan answered the Lord, and said: from going to and fro in the earth, and from walking

> up and down in it. And the Lord said unto Satan, Hast thou considered my servant Job, that there is none like him in the earth, a perfect and an upright man, one that feareth God, and escheweth evil? Then, Satan answered the Lord, and said, Doth Job fear God for nought? Hast not thou made an hedge about him, and about his house, and about all that he hath on every side? Thou hast blessed the work of his hands, and his substance is increased in the land.
>
> But put forth thine hand now, and touch all that he hath, and he will curse thee to thy face. And the Lord said unto Satan, Behold, all that he hath is in thy power; only upon himself put not forth thine hand. So, Satan went forth from the presence of the Lord (Job 1:1-12 KJV).

Another essential tool in overcoming failure is thinking positively. Negativity is the mother of pessimism which in turn begets discouragement and dejection. When we feed our minds only with negative thoughts, the outcome is drastic, we down play our personal efforts and this creates fears and anxiety and the mind can no longer function positively. One begins to see a red label where there is a green one; he or she sees black where there is white because the mind can only reproduce what is given to it. Obscurity damps the eyes of the mind and retards its productivity. Sometimes, it is good to apply what may be called an "phenomenological epoche' (a bracketing of all the unnecessary judgments and prejudices) in Epistemology. Societal judgments and prejudices are silent mental killers. Every positive mind should try as much as possible to avoid them.

Positivity is a mother of invention. It leads to positive exploits, positive activities and historic attainments. Positive thinking is a healer of agony and distress. It is a grand and underground worker. It pierces every darkened image to create and manufacture thinking materials for societal building. Moreover, nothing is impossible before God.

It is good to state also that our mind should be child-like mind where there is no impurity, greedy and so on, it should be sacred where our Lord God can find His home. There is a common belief among Catholics that the first tabernacle where the Lord dwelled on Earth was the womb of Her blessed Mother, Mary whose heart prepared a soft and sacred landing for Him. Mary's heart is pure and sacred like that of her child – Jesus, it is seat of holiness and acceptance.

3.3 Breaking the Darkened Yoke and Grazing in Light

One good thing about life is that it presents us with options. Children cannot choose but once one reaches the age of maturity or reasoning he or she can choose between good and evil, between life and death, between God and Satan.

However, it is challenging to choose, to be able to make a right choice. Some are living in bondage today due to the type of choice they make. Wrong choices in life can lead to a darkened yoke. Even difficulties we encounter on our life journey can become darkened yokes that are difficult to crack. Thus, life challenges present us darkened yokes which when not managed very well can lead to despair and psychological breakdown. I once listened with keen interest to the story of a father of five children in Europe who wanted to abandon his family and run away because he lost his job. Life became a hard nut to crack for him until we met each other few years ago in train from Italy to Germany. My little advice and mental counselling helped him to regain his doddering, wobbling and tottering state. God was at the center of our discussion of course and the need to choose the yoke of God which makes the difference from other yokes. In fact, the Lord was emphatic about this: take my yoke upon you and learn from me, for I am gentle and humble in heart, and you will find rest for your souls, for my yoke is easy and my burden is light (Matthew 11: 29-30).

Satan presents us always with alluring, charming and enticing pictures which are pleasant to the eyes in order to deceive the mind but almost 100 percent of those glaring materials are scam and charlatanic. Satan has no free gift. His gifts are darkened yokes which can destroy man physically, socially and psychologically. It is like a Cankerworm which eats deep into the bone marrow and causes health hazards. Thus, we must apply caution and anchor our faith in God to resist the tricky activities of the evil one.

Faith in God helps a lot to break through darkened yokes and enable an easy grazing in light. Anyone who is a prayer warrior will find it hard to fall prey to satanic intellectual prowess. That is why the Scripture asks us to pray in and out of season because the enemy is on daily rampage (2 Timothy 4) and one of the Christian songs has it that in the "presence of God anointing breaks the yoke." It goes thus:

> When I come into Your presence I'm
> so happy.
> I'm so happy
> When I come into Your presence I'm
> so glad.
> So glad
> In Your presence there is anointing
> Your Spirit moves within me
> In Your presence
> The anointing breaks the yoke

breaks the yoke
When I come into Your presence I'm
so happy.
I'm so happy
When I come into Your presence I'm
so glad.
So glad
In Your presence there is anointing
Your Spirit moves within me
In Your presence
The anointing breaks the yoke

Having a breakthrough in difficult times is possible and grazing and making merry amidst darkened yokes of life is possible too. All we need is grace. It is called the "enabling power" to attain perfection and graze freely with no iota of fear. Grace "enables the recipient to do and to be what he or she cannot do and cannot be if left to his or her own means." We need such enabling power to survive hardships and posses our possession. Many believers have broken through a tough and bewildering situation through Grace. Daniel survived in the den of Lions through Grace (cf. Daniel 1 ff) and Queen Esther became a queen through Grace (cf. Esther 1 ff). Grace is the key to breakthroughs and is a weapon of the weapon of the weak in God. Whosoever wants to be a winner must grab it.

CHAPTER FOUR

KEEPING OUR GOALS ALIVE

4.1 Born to Win

Philosophically, man is a hylemorphic being. He is composed of matter and form and what man conceives in potency through personal efforts and divine intervention comes to actuality. We are all born to win. Yes, we have capabilities and qualities that are innate in man. It is left for man to put them into motion or bury them underground like the ungrateful servant in the Bible. May be a glance on the parable of the talents in the Bible will throw more light on this:

> A rich man delegates the management of his wealth to his servants, much as investors in today's markets do. He gives five talents (a large unit of money) to the first servant, two talents to the second, and one talent to the third. Two of the servants earn 100 percent returns by trading with the funds, but the third servant hides the money in the ground and earns nothing. The rich man returns, rewards the two who made money, but severely punishes the servant who did nothing (Mathew 25: 14-30).

This means that we are all gifted. We have all it takes. It is good to know from the foregoing that God is interested in our productivity. He wants us to be productive. It is the enemy that discourages us and instills us with wrong reasoning. I like using testimonies to support my stand.

In the course of my stay in Italy, I met a young promising couple who started life with one bus but today they own a Limited Liability Company.

They have extended their tentacles to many other viable business areas of life. Initially, the wife was an obstacle. She was afraid of failure and bankruptcy but I was on their neck. I opened the woman's eyes to the mystery of God who never disappoints but appoints; who never deceives but establishes and her dwindling faith was revitalized. Today she is a woman of faith and a motivator.

We should not forget that we are "imago Dei." We are created in God's image and likeness (cf. Gen 1: 26). We are little gods. Therefore, if we believe in ourselves and believe in the creator we will record many achievements like him. Interestingly, those who fly to the moon, who build or construct or invent electronic accessories for our use, are all humans like us. It is high time we believed in ourselves, in our intellectual acumen and prowess and shame the devil that is a liar and deceiver and would like to draw many to his ugly part. His time is almost up. He is now struggling to draw souls to himself by showing darkness where there is light, desperation where there is hope. We need to wake up or resurrect from our slumber and face the reality of life squarely. Life is good because the Creator Himself is the "*summum Bonum*" (Absolute Goodness) and we see it in His creation. In this regard St Augustine asserts:

> Question the beauty of the earth, question the beauty of the sea, question the beauty of the air, amply spread around everywhere, question the beauty of the sky, question the serried ranks of the stars, question the sun making the day glorious with its bright beams, question the moon tempering the darkness of the following night with its shining rays, question the animals that move in the waters, that amble about on dry land, that fly in the air; their souls hidden, their bodies evident; the visible bodies needing to be controlled, the invisible souls controlling them; question all these things. They all answer you, 'Here we are, look; we're beautiful.' Their beauty is their confession. Who made these

> beautiful changeable things, if not one
> who is beautiful and unchangeable?[12]

Therefore, we need to fulfill the Lord's injunction of winning the world. He died and resurrected. We need to resurrect suit.

4.2 The Resurrected Man

After the death of Christ, the disciples were afraid of the Jews, they were afraid of dying and of being killed by the Jews. Those who killed their master above all were disappointed and went back to their various jobs. For them their mission was over.

Initially, they thought that Jesus was a warrior who would have defeated and killed all His enemies. Little wonder, Jesus asked them a vital question when they got to the Region of Caesarea Philippi: "who do people say the son of man is? They replied: some say John the Baptist; others say Elijah; and others still, Jeremiah or one of the prophets…. (cf. Matthew 16). They were naïve and ignorant of whom He was. Thus,

---

[12] St Augustine Sermon' 241 Easter: C. 411 A.D.

seeing their great master who was once commanding demons, who was commanding the waves of the sea and they obeyed him, being humiliated, insulted and killed like a thief, they thought it was their end. They were hopeless, distressed and dejected. This is seen in the discussion of two desperate disciples on their way to Emmaus:

> That very day two of them were going to a village named Emma'us, about seven miles from Jerusalem, and talking with each other about all these things that had happened. While they were talking and discussing together, Jesus himself drew near and went with them. But their eyes were kept from recognizing him. And he said to them, "What is this conversation which you are holding with each other as you walk?" And they stood still, looking sad. Then one of them, named Cle'opas, answered him, "Are you the only visitor to Jerusalem who does not know the things that have

happened there in these days?" And he said to them, "What things?" And they said to him, "Concerning Jesus of Nazareth, who was a prophet mighty in deed and word before God and all the people, and how our chief priests and rulers delivered him up to be condemned to death, and crucified him. But we had hoped that he was the one to redeem Israel. Yes, and besides all this, it is now the third day since this happened. Moreover, some women of our company amazed us. They were at the tomb early in the morning and did not find his body; and they came back saying that they had even seen a vision of angels, who said that he was alive. Some of those who were with us went to the tomb, and found it just as the women had said; but him they did not see." (Lk 24: 13-24 RSV).

They were struggling with anguish and desperation while the resurrected man was with them. Their eyes were darkened because they lacked faith and were following Jesus for vain glory. They thought he wouldn't have died.

Human Ego needs to be tamed if we need to walk with the resurrected man. It needs to be tamed from the things of this world which are ephemeral, fleeting and fugitive. Little wonder the scripture insists that you seek first the kingdom of God and his righteousness, and all these things will be added to you (cf. Matthew 6:33).

The resurrected man in our context here means the new man, the fearless man, the man full of knowledge and fear of God. The sons of the resurrection are the sons of light. Just as darkness couldn't hold Jesus siege in the grave, so also the sons of the resurrection are victorious over darkness. They are sons of the Pentecost, dauntless, fearless and resolute in their actions. They may speak different languages. Yet they are united and have a common goal – joining their master in heaven.

4.3 Heaven Our Last Bus Stop

Some have argued that heaven is not real; that it is a scam, while religion is seen as the opium of the people by Karl Marx. Some even think that religion is an instrument used by the strong to keep the weak down. Those who believe in religion are seen as blindfolded and are battling with ignorance. Even the famous axiom, "Christ will come soon repent" has been down-trodden and bastardized because it is an ancient axiom. They argue that right from time immemorial the tale has been there and people have thrown in faith, given up their evil ways, sold off their belongings yet Christ is nowhere to be seen.

Many people are no longer afraid to hear of the "*parousia*" (the second coming of Christ). For them, it is also a scam. Some now believe in the survival of the fittest while some bury themselves in the vices of gluttony, binge eating and drinking. They say, let us eat and drink today, for tomorrow we may die. According to them, the thought of Jesus' second coming is an optical illusion and could be explained as manmade. Those who believe in rapture are seen as suffering from psychosomatic illnesses. They are charlatanic in their thinking and need psychotherapy for healing.

However, can the above affirmation be real, that heaven is an utopian idea? Personally, I consider such thoughts as false. Most of these thinkers are already agents of darkness seeking for weak souls to lead to perdition.

Heaven is real my dear noble reader. I know a man who died and resurrected after three days – the only in human history. He testifies to the world with His life history that heaven is real. That man is Jesus. His life history testifies to this. When we read the event of transfiguration for example, we will deduct a lot from the scene. Jesus went up to the Mountain with Peter, James and John, sons of Zebede. I call these three persons, the people of inner circle. They knew a lot about the master Jesus. They were also people struggling to be the first or have an honorable position in his kingdom, thinking that everything ends in this world. They wanted to be king makers in His kingdom. Jesus wanted to show them the foretaste of His glory. In other words, they had the glimpse of heaven. Peter saw it and exclaimed, Master it is good for us to be here. If you like, I will make 3 tents: one for you, one for Moses and one for Elijah. Let us cast a glance on this epoch making event:

> "And after six days Jesus took with him Peter and James and John his brother, and led them up a high mountain apart. And he was transfigured before them, and his face shone like the sun, and his garments became white as light. And behold, there appeared to them Moses and Eli'jah, talking with him. And Peter said to Jesus, "Lord, it is well that we are here; if you wish, I will make three booths here, one for you and one for Moses and one for Eli'jah." He was still speaking, when lo, a bright cloud overshadowed them, and a voice from the cloud said, "This is my beloved Son, with whom I am well pleased; listen to him." When the disciples heard this, they fell on their faces, and were filled with awe. But Jesus came and touched them,

> saying, "Rise, and have no fear." And when they lifted up their eyes, they saw no one but Jesus only. (Matthew 17:1-8 RSV).

In this scene, our fathers in faith, Moses and Elijah were seen. They died many years ago, but they were seen because they are in God's glory – heaven. Another evidence is the ascension of our Lord. Jesus ascended, not into nothing but into heaven where He is seated at the right hand of the father and intercedes for us. In this regard, the scripture declares: "Then he led them out as far as Bethany, and lifting up his hands he blessed them. While he blessed them, he parted from them, and was carried up into heaven. And they returned to Jerusalem with great joy, and were continually in the temple blessing God. (cf. Lk 24:50 RSV)

Therefore, Ascension is not a return to nothing as I mentioned above but an upward slope into heaven where the God-man has gone to prepare a place for us. Thus, heaven is the final bus stop for believers. Our lives cannot be lived only in this world. They are open to eternity. We are children of the eternal father, whom he awaits in His glorious heaven.

CONCLUSION

From the foregoing, we have been able to expose the concept of light and darkness and have made a historic and handy record of grazing in light amidst darkness. I call it a handbook, a "*vademecum*" that will guard and guide our steps towards a perfective inheritance in heaven and a healthier mental state.

It has proven the candid truth that God exists and He is the primary source of light. Whoever accepts Him walks in light and darkness has no power over him. He so much loves the world that he sent his only begotten son that whoever believes in Him might not perish but might have the light of life (cf. Jn 3: 16). God's love for man has no measure. It is limitless and without condition. It is a total self – giving. He protects and promotes us when we graze in darkness amidst lions and wolves, amidst valley and hills. He is our shepherd and whoever grazes in light lacks nothing.

However, if we must work with the Lord, we must have a change of mindset, because a wrong mindset sets our holy plans ablaze and draws our good deeds and plans into oblivion. The mind, as I mentioned above, is a shape element of human productive and nervous system. It is at the center of human activities and it is a positive energy that functions psychologically, socio-religiously and other wise. It needs to be guarded with caution. We need to invite God to take hold of our minds every now and then. We need to establish a strong rapport with Him. If God dwells in our hearts, He will sanitize and sanctify them and make them His own.

I must also state that this book did not exhaust all the ideas on grazing in light amidst darkness. There are a whole lot of things to be said on this aspect. It is only a pathfinder, an idealistic human explorer that is subject to constructive criticism because no man is "*scit omnia*" (all knowing). I stand to be corrected positively. All my effort is to help to see how the situation of human agony and distress may be ameliorated by establishing the fact God exists. Heaven is also real and human sufferings are attributed to the ancient tempter who is absolute darkness.

Meanwhile, human suffering can be short-lived at times if we have patience, trust God and have correct mindsets. Mental transformation and strong will can be sources of strength in fighting darkness and human suffering. Satan hardly penetrates a faithful, energetic and spiritual mind.

Conclusively, let us try to be God fearing, positive and optimistic thinkers. We will see that things which seem to be impossible will be possible for us and we will enjoy a better world privy of fear and psycho-religious torments which are the bane of human upliftment and rejuvenation.

Printed in the United States
by Baker & Taylor Publisher Services